GEO

Apostrophe

Mary Elizabeth Salzmann

Published by SandCastle™, an imprint of ABDO Publishing Company, 4940 Viking Drive, Edina, Minnesota 55435.

Printed in the United States.

Photo credits: PhotoDisc

Library of Congress Cataloging-in-Publication Data

Salzmann, Mary Elizabeth, 1968-
    Apostrophe / Mary Elizabeth Salzmann.
        p. cm. -- (Punctuation)
    Includes index.
    ISBN 1-57765-625-3
        1. English language--Punctuation--Juvenile literature. 2. Apostrophe--Juvenile
literature. [1. English language--Punctuation. 2. Apostrophe.] I. Title.

PE1450 .S23 2001
428.1--dc21
                                                                                2001022898

The SandCastle concept, content, and reading method have been reviewed and approved by a national advisory board including literacy specialists, librarians, elementary school teachers, early childhood education professionals, and parents.

Let Us Know

After reading the book, SandCastle would like you to tell us your stories about reading. What is your favorite page? Was there something hard that you needed help with? Share the ups and downs of learning to read. We want to hear from you! To get posted on the ABDO Publishing Company Web site, send us email at:

sandcastle@abdopub.com

About SandCastle™

Nonfiction books for the beginning reader

- Basic concepts of phonics are incorporated with integrated language methods of reading instruction. Most words are short, and phrases, letter sounds, and word sounds are repeated.

- Readability is determined by the number of words in each sentence, the number of characters in each word, and word lists based on curriculum frameworks.

- Full-color photography reinforces word meanings and concepts.

- "Words I Can Read" list at the end of each book teaches basic elements of grammar, helps the reader recognize the words in the text, and builds vocabulary.

- Reading levels are indicated by the number of flags on the castle.

Look for more SandCastle books in these three reading levels:

Level 1 (one flag)	**Level 2** (two flags)	**Level 3** (three flags)

Grades Pre-K to K 5 or fewer words per page	**Grades K to 1** 5 to 10 words per page	**Grades 1 to 2** 10 to 15 words per page

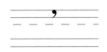

This is an **apostrophe**.

I know when to use **apostrophes**.

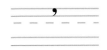

Apostrophes are used to write about something that belongs to someone.

Sandra's hair is braided.

The **apostrophe** is used with the letter "s."

Andre is tipping over Ben's raft.

Matt is on Stefan's
baseball team.

Their team's name is the
Blue Jays.

An **apostrophe** can make two words into one.

I am laughing because I'm happy.

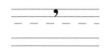

The **apostrophe** takes the place of missing letters.

They're best friends.

The word with the **apostrophe** is called a contraction.

She's playing dress up.

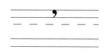

Jenna's dad is helping her learn how to ride a bicycle.

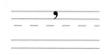

Becky is at the beach.

What color is Becky's swimsuit?

(pink)

Words I Can Read

Nouns

A noun is a person, place, or thing

apostrophe
(uh-POSS-truh-fee)
pp. 5, 9, 13, 15, 17

apostrophes
(uh-POSS-truh-feez)
pp. 5, 7

baseball team
(BAYSS-bawl TEEM)
p. 11

beach (BEECH) p. 21

bicycle (BYE-si-kuhl) p. 19

color (KUHL-ur) p. 21

contraction
(kuhn-TRAK-shun) p. 17

dad (DAD) p. 19

dress up (DRESS UHP)
p. 17

friends (FRENDZ) p. 15

hair (HAIR) p. 7

letter (LET-ur) p. 9

letters (LET-urz) p. 15

name (NAYM) p. 11

pink (PINGK) p. 21

place (PLAYSS) p. 15

raft (RAFT) p. 9

s (ESS) p. 9

swimsuit (SWIM-soot)
p. 21

word (WURD) p. 17

words (WURDZ) p. 13

Proper Nouns

A proper noun is the name of a person, place, or thing

Andre (AHN-dray) p. 9

Becky (BEK-ee) p. 21

Blue Jays (BLOO JAYZ)
p. 11

Matt (MAT) p. 11

Pronouns

A pronoun is a word that replaces a noun

her (HUR) p. 19

I (EYE) pp. 5, 13

someone (SUHM-wuhn)
p. 7

something (SUHM-thing)
p. 7

this (THISS) p. 5

what (WUHT) p. 21

Verbs
A verb is an action or being word

am (AM) p. 13
are (AR) p. 7
belongs (bi-LONGZ) p. 7
called (KAWLD) p. 17
can (KAN) p. 13
helping (HELP-ing) p. 19

is (IZ)
  pp. 5, 7, 9, 11, 17, 19, 21
know (NOH) p. 5
laughing (LAF-ing) p. 13
learn (LURN) p. 19
make (MAKE) p. 13
playing (PLAY-ing) p. 17

ride (RIDE) p. 19
takes (TAYKSS) p. 15
tipping (TIP-ing) p. 9
use (YOOZ) p. 5
used (YOOZD) pp. 7, 9
write (RITE) p. 7

Adjectives
An adjective describes something

Becky's (BECK-eez) p. 21
Ben's (BENZ) p. 9
best (BEST) p. 15
braided (BRAYD-ed) p. 7
happy (HAP-ee) p. 13

Jenna's (JE-nuhz) p. 19
missing (MISS-ing) p. 15
one (WUHN) p. 13
Sandra's (SAND-ruhz) p. 7
Stefan's (STEF-ahnz) p. 11

team's (TEEMZ) p. 11
their (THAIR) p. 11
two (TOO) p. 13

Adverbs
An adverb tells how, when, or where something happens

how (HOU) p. 19

over (OH-vur) p. 9

Contractions
A contraction is two words combined with an apostrophe

I'm (EYEM) p. 13

she's (SHEEZ) p. 17

they're (THAIR) p. 15

23

Glossary

bicycle – a vehicle with two wheels, a seat, handlebars to steer with, and pedals that you push with your feet

braided – divided into several parts that are woven together

contraction – words combined by replacing letters with an apostrophe

raft – a flat boat or mat used to float on water

swimsuit – the clothes you wear when you go swimming